Flitterific Story

Read the story, then flip the book over
to find some magical activities!

PaRragon

Bath · New York · Singapore · Hong Kong · Cologne · Delhi
Melbourne · Amsterdam · Johannesburg · Auckland · Shenzhen

First published by Parragon in 2012
Parragon
Queen Street House
4 Queen Street
Bath BA1 1HE, UK
www.parragon.com

Edited by Samantha Crockford
Designed by Karl Tall
Production by Sarah Brown

ISBN 978-1-4454-4802-2

Printed in China

TinkerBell
AND THE
GREAT FAIRY RESCUE

PaRragon

Bath • New York • Singapore • Hong Kong • Cologne • Delhi
Melbourne • Amsterdam • Johannesburg • Auckland • Shenzhen

Tinker Bell and her fairy friends from Pixie Hollow were on their way to bring summer to the mainland!

Summer needed the fairies' constant attention – which meant that Tink was going to be on the mainland for months instead of days. She was very excited!

Tink and her friend Terence, a dust-keeper fairy, landed in a clearing.
Terence walked over to a huge oak tree and pulled back a thick tangle of leaves.

"Wow!" cried Tink. Hidden beneath the tree was fairy camp – an entire fairy
community bustling with activity.

Just then, a loud *CRACK!* went through the fairy camp! The noise made Fawn,
an animal fairy, jump. She knocked over some paint and splattered a butterfly's wing.
The butterfly flew off!

Tinker Bell was curious. She flew out of camp to find out what had made the loud noise – it was a car! She followed it down the road to a human house.

"Tinker Bell!" Vidia cried. She couldn't believe Tink would do something so dangerous! The fairies knew they should stay hidden from humans.

After the humans had gone into their house, Tink flew down to examine the car. "This is amazing!" she said.

Inside the engine, Tink found a handle and turned it. She didn't know that each turn of the handle was showering Vidia with water! Vidia wasn't impressed – she couldn't fly with wet wings.

Just then, the door to the house opened and out walked a little girl called Lizzy and her father, Dr Griffiths. Tink and Vidia froze, but they didn't need to worry. The humans were looking at a butterfly – the one that had been splattered with paint!

"The wings have two entirely different patterns," Dr Griffiths observed.

"Well, I guess that's just the way the fairies decided to paint it," Lizzy said.

"Fairies do not paint butterfly wings, because as you know, fairies are not real," her father declared as he placed the butterfly in a jar.

After the humans left, Tink and Vidia went exploring.

"Wow!" said Tink. She landed next to a row of buttons lined up like stepping stones. "These will be perfect for the new wagon prototype I've been working on."

"I'm not carrying this human junk back to camp..." began Vidia, but then she spotted something that made her stop in her tracks. It was a little fairy house that Lizzy had built!

Vidia wanted to leave, but Tinker Bell headed straight for the house.

Tink went inside of the house, ignoring Vidia's reminders that humans could be dangerous. Frustrated at Tinker Bell, Vidia whipped up a gust of wind that slammed the door shut.

Tink didn't mind. She was having fun discovering the tiny house's gadgets.

But suddenly, Vidia saw Lizzy approaching in the distance. She pulled on the door to let Tink out, but it was jammed shut!

Vidia hid, watching as Lizzy got closer. "Oh, no! What have I done!" she cried as she watched Lizzy peer into the house.

"A ... a ... a fairy," Lizzy whispered in astonishment. Finally, she had proof that fairies were real! She started running back home, while Tinker Bell bounced around inside of the fairy house.

Lizzy went upstairs to her bedroom and peeked inside the fairy house. But Tinker Bell was nowhere to be seen.

"Where have you gone?" wondered Lizzy. She took the roof off the house and *ZIP!* Tink darted out. Mr Twitches, the family cat, immediately lunged for the fairy! Lizzy quickly put Tinker Bell in a birdcage to keep her safe. Vidia watched at the window – she thought Lizzy was taking Tink prisoner.

Vidia knew that she had to free Tinker Bell, but she couldn't do it alone.
Now that her wings were dry, she flew back to the fairy camp to get help. As Vidia
explained to her friends what had happened, a rain storm started!

"We can't fly in the rain," Fawn said. "And the meadow is already flooded!"

Clank and Bobble had a plan. They would build a boat!

Back at the humans' house, Lizzy let Tinker Bell out of the birdcage.

"You don't have to be scared," said Lizzy. "I'm very nice. Look, I've been drawing fairies all my life."

Tinker Bell was amazed by Lizzy's collection of fairy pictures. But the little girl had her fairy facts all wrong! Tink tried to tell Lizzy, but all Lizzy heard was a jingling sound. With some hand movements and a little bit of pointing, Tink finally told Lizzy her name.

"Tinker Bell?" Lizzy cried. "What a lovely name!"

Tinker Bell pointed to the window.

"You want to go?" asked Lizzy. "I understand." She went to the window and opened it wide. Tink made it as far as the windowsill and stopped. It was pouring outside!

"Can't you fly in the rain?" guessed Lizzy. "You can stay with me until it stops. Then you can teach me more about fairies!"

Tinker Bell decided she might as well. "The only way I could get back to fairy camp now is if I had a boat," she thought.

The other fairies *did* have a boat! But the rescuers were heading straight for a waterfall! Thinking quickly, Vidia hovered in front of the boat and created a burst of wind. The boat started to turn around! But then raindrops soaked Vidia's wings and she had to stop. The boat was swept towards the waterfall again.

"Hang on, we're going straight down!" yelled Bobble.

At the last second, Silvermist made the water rise up so that the drop wasn't as steep. The boat crashed onshore, but the fairies were all right.

"I guess our sailing days are over," said Bobble.

Back at the house, Tink and Lizzy created a Fairy Field Guide, filled with fairy facts. By the time they had finished, the rain was stopping. It was time for Tink to go home. As much as she was going to miss the little girl, Tink wanted to get back to her fairy friends.

But as Tinker Bell was about to leave, she saw Lizzy trying to show her father the Fairy Field Guide. But Dr Griffiths was too busy trying to fix the leaks in the roof to listen. Tink realized she had to help Lizzy and her father spend time together.

When Tink flew back into Lizzy's bedroom, the look of joy on Lizzy's face let Tink know that coming back had been the right thing to do.

Lizzy went to sleep and Tinker Bell watched as Dr Griffiths came up to check on her.

"There just aren't enough hours in the day," he said to his daughter. It warmed Tink's heart, and she felt even more determined to find a way to help them.

Meanwhile, the other fairies were continuing their mission to find Tink on foot. Vidia spotted the muddy road that led to Lizzy's house. Vidia helped her friends across, but then got stuck in the mud herself. Silvermist, Fawn, Rosetta and Iridessa grabbed onto her and pulled, but she wouldn't budge.

The fairies suddenly spotted a car coming straight at them! Luckily, Iridessa saved them by reflecting the light from the car's headlights. The driver got out of his car. "Hello? Is somebody out there?" he asked.

Fawn grabbed his shoelace and instructed the others to hold on tight. When the driver turned to leave, they were all pulled out of the mud!

Back at the house, Tinker Bell had an idea! She secretly fixed all of the leaks in the house for Dr Griffiths, so he could spend more time with Lizzy.

But then Tink noticed the paint-splattered butterfly in a jar on Dr Griffiths's desk. It made Tink feel terrible to see the poor creature trapped, so she set it free.

Later, Lizzy went to show her father her Fairy Field Guide. But Dr Griffiths was upset.

"The butterfly is gone," he announced. "There is no one else in this house, there's only one logical explanation. It must have been you."

"I didn't," replied Lizzy. "It must have been …"

"It must have been who?" Dr Griffiths asked.

"I could tell you, Father," Lizzy declared. "But you wouldn't believe me."

"Very well," Dr Griffiths said, "off to your room. I'm very disappointed with you."

Back in Lizzy's room, Tinker Bell apologized for getting the girl into trouble.
"I'm glad you're here," Lizzy told Tink. "You're my best friend. I wish I were a fairy just like you. Then I could fly around with the other fairies all the time."

That gave Tinker Bell an idea! She told Lizzy to close her eyes and spread out her arms. Then she hovered above Lizzy's head and showered it with pixie dust. It was time for some flying lessons!

Downstairs, a door creaked open.

"All clear," announced Iridessa. The fairies entered the kitchen.

"Okay," began Vidia. "Tinker Bell is upstairs. The little girl has her in a cage. There's also a large human in the house who doesn't like creatures with wings."

The fairies looked at each other in alarm.

"Great!" Fawn exclaimed. "Anything else?"

But before Vidia could reply, the fairies had their answer. Mr Twitches was standing in the doorway!

Meanwhile, Dr Griffiths heard strange noises coming from upstairs. He went to investigate. Lizzy tried to act normal, but the pixie dust hadn't worn off yet. She had to hold onto the furniture to stop herself from floating off the floor.

"How did you get footprints on the ceiling?" her father asked.

"Well, I ..." began Lizzy. "I was flying. My fairy showed me how."

"You've got to stop this nonsense!" Dr Griffiths insisted. "I believe in what is real... and it's about time you started doing the same."

Tinker Bell had had enough. She flew straight into the face of Dr Griffiths!

While the other fairies distracted Mr Twitches downstairs, Vidia headed upstairs to save Tinker Bell. Vidia got there just as Tink revealed herself to Lizzy's father. Dr Griffiths tried to catch Tink, but Vidia pushed her out of the way. Dr Griffiths caught Vidia instead!

"I must get this to the museum right away!" declared Dr Griffiths as he ran out of the house with Vidia in a jar.

"Please, wait!" Lizzy begged, following him outside. But Lizzy wasn't able to stop her father.

The other fairies had tamed Mr Twitches with some catnip that Rosetta and
Fawn found. They rode on the now friendly cat up to Lizzy's room. Tinker Bell and
Lizzy were trying to figure out how to get Dr Griffiths to release Vidia.

Tinker Bell was happy to see her friends again, but now it was her turn to try and
save Vidia. But it was still raining.

"How are we going to get there?" Fawn asked.

"We can't fly," said Tink, "but I think I know somebody who can."

Lizzy was nervous as the fairies bundled her up in a rain coat and hat. "Floating around my room is one thing," she told Tinker Bell, "but flying all the way to London...."

Tink looked at her friend as if to say, "You can do it!" That was enough for Lizzy.

The fairies swirled around Lizzy and showered her with pixie dust.

"All aboard!" cried Tinker Bell.

Tink settled under Lizzy's collar while the other fairies tucked themselves into
her raincoat pockets. Lizzy had a rough start, but was soon flying smoothly above the
country road that led to the city.

A little while later, the magnificent sight of London came into view.

Once they got closer, Tinker Bell flew into the car's engine and made it stop.

Inside the car, Dr Griffiths banged on the steering wheel. "No, no, no, no, no!" he cried in frustration. He climbed out of the car.

"Father!" Lizzy called. Dr Griffiths turned to see his daughter flying towards him, pixie dust trailing behind her.

Dr Griffiths couldn't believe his eyes! "How are you doing that?" he asked. "There's no feasible scientific explanation. It has to be... magic."

Lizzy smiled. "It is magic," she told him.

"But where does it come from?" Dr Griffiths wondered.

"Fairies," answered Lizzy. "Some things are not meant to be seen."

Suddenly, her father understood. "You're right," he agreed, "just believed."

He handed the jar to Lizzy. Seconds later, Vidia was reunited with her friends.
Then everyone – including Dr Griffiths – headed back to the country, with the help
of a generous sprinkling of pixie dust.

A few days later, Tink and Vidia sat together, sipping their tea. Not only did they know each other better now – but they had actually become good friends.

As they watched Lizzy and Dr Griffiths, they could see that father and daughter were getting to know each other better, too.

"Beautiful sight, isn't it?" asked Vidia.

"Nothing more beautiful in the whole wide world," Tink agreed.

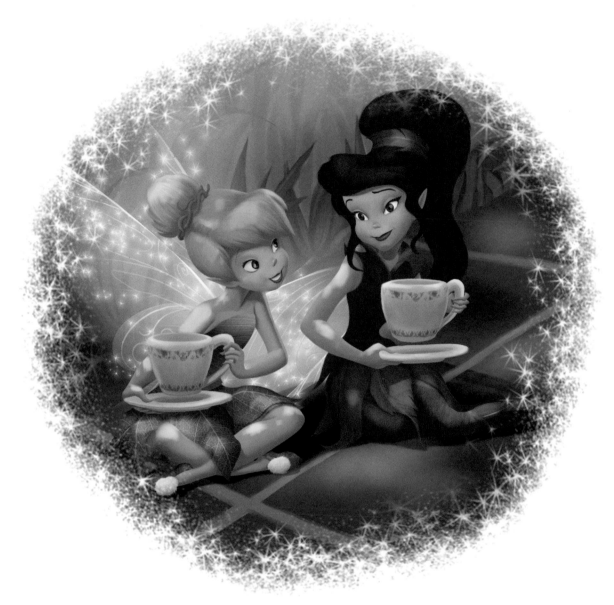

The End

Now close the book
and *flip it over* to find some
magical fairy activities!

Magical Activities

Complete the activities, then flip the book
over to read a flitterific story!

PaRRagon

Bath • New York • Singapore • Hong Kong • Cologne • Delhi
Melbourne • Amsterdam • Johannesburg • Auckland • Shenzhen

Welcome to Pixie Hollow

"These things will help you find your talent," Queen Clarion explains to new arrival, Tinker Bell.

Colour this picture.

2

Fairy friends

The other fairies can't wait to show Tinker Bell their magical talents! Colour their pictures.

Do you know what these fairies' special talents are? Turn the page to find out!

Silvermist

Fawn

Iridessa

Rosetta

Fairy talents

Use the code to discover each of these fairies' unique talents.

t r e l a w g i h n m d

Silvermist is a _ _ _ _ _ fairy.

Iridessa is a _ _ _ _ _ fairy.

Fawn is an _ _ _ _ _ _ fairy.

Rosetta is a _ _ _ _ _ _ fairy.

Answers on page 31

Draw Tinker Bell

Tinker Bell
is a tinker fairy. She loves
to fix things and
is very good at it.

Using the grid
as a guide, draw your
own picture of the
clever tinker fairy.

Spot the difference

Test your talent for spotting things. Look at these two pictures of the fairy friends, and circle five differences in the second image.

Answers on page 31

Your fairy name

The fairies in Pixie Hollow all have magical names. Find out your fairy name by following these simple steps!

1. Write down your birthday in numbers. For example: 23 – 6 – 04

2. Add the numbers together. For example: 23 + 6 + 4 = 33

3. If you still have two numbers, add them together until you are left with just one number. For example: 3 + 3 = 6

4. Look at the name list and match your number to your fairy name!

1. Moon Shimmer
2. Willow Fly
3. Feather Tree
4. Sun Beam
5. Frosty Mist
6. Rainbow Ray
7. Ember Glow
8. Meadow Nettle
9. Glitter Wing

My fairy name is...

_____

Odd fairy out

Rosetta loves putting pretty flowers in her hair. Which of these pictures is slightly different from the others?

1

2

3

4

5

6

Answers on page 31

8

Find Iridessa

How many times can you find the name IRIDESSA in the puzzle below? Look forwards, backwards, up, down and diagonally.

I	Q	R	G	A	V	M	J	K	U	L
R	R	Y	A	S	S	E	D	I	R	I
I	H	I	B	E	W	F	X	Q	R	R
D	N	A	D	Y	F	K	A	I	A	I
E	M	S	K	E	T	S	D	C	S	D
S	W	S	S	S	S	E	V	T	S	E
S	O	E	S	E	S	S	Y	K	E	S
A	G	D	D	S	C	Z	A	R	D	S
J	T	I	A	J	H	Y	N	O	I	A
K	R	R	A	S	S	E	D	I	R	I
I	B	I	R	I	D	E	S	S	A	H

Number of Iridessas:

Answers on page 31

9

Tink's special moment

Tinker Bell is chosen to make the autumn sceptre. This holds the precious moonstone and will help to restore the Pixie Dust Tree at the end of autumn.

Colour this picture.

Tink's workshop

Tinker Bell is busy in her workshop, designing the autumn spectre.

Can you find four things in the picture that begin with the letter 'C'?

Colour this picture.

Answers on page 31

11

The lost treasure

Tink has accidentally broken the moonstone! She needs to find the Mirror of Incanta, which can grant her a wish.

Can you help Tink through the maze to the magical mirror?

Answers on page 31

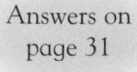

Tinker teamwork

In the end,
Terence helps Tinker
Bell to build a beautiful
spectre, dotted with the
pieces of sparkling
moonstone.

*Colour this
picture.*

Fairy squares

Play this game with a friend!

Take turns to draw one line between two dots, horizontally or vertically. If you complete a box on your turn, put your initials inside it.

When the grid is full, the person with the most squares wins!

14

Your fairy style

Each of the fairies has her very own style. What would yours be? Draw yourself as a fairy in the frame.

Hint: Think about what colour your dress would be, how you would wear your hair, and what tools would help you in your unique talent.

Time for summer

It's time for the fairies to bring summer to the mainland! Tink is flying to Fairy Camp with her friend Terence.

Colour this picture.

16

Pixie pathways

Tink needs to join her friends at Fairy Camp. Can you help her choose the correct path?

D

C

A   B

Answers on page 31

17

Memory game

Tink and Terence arrive at Fairy Camp and there's a lot to take in!

Look carefully at this picture, then turn the page and see if you can answer the questions – using only your memory!

18

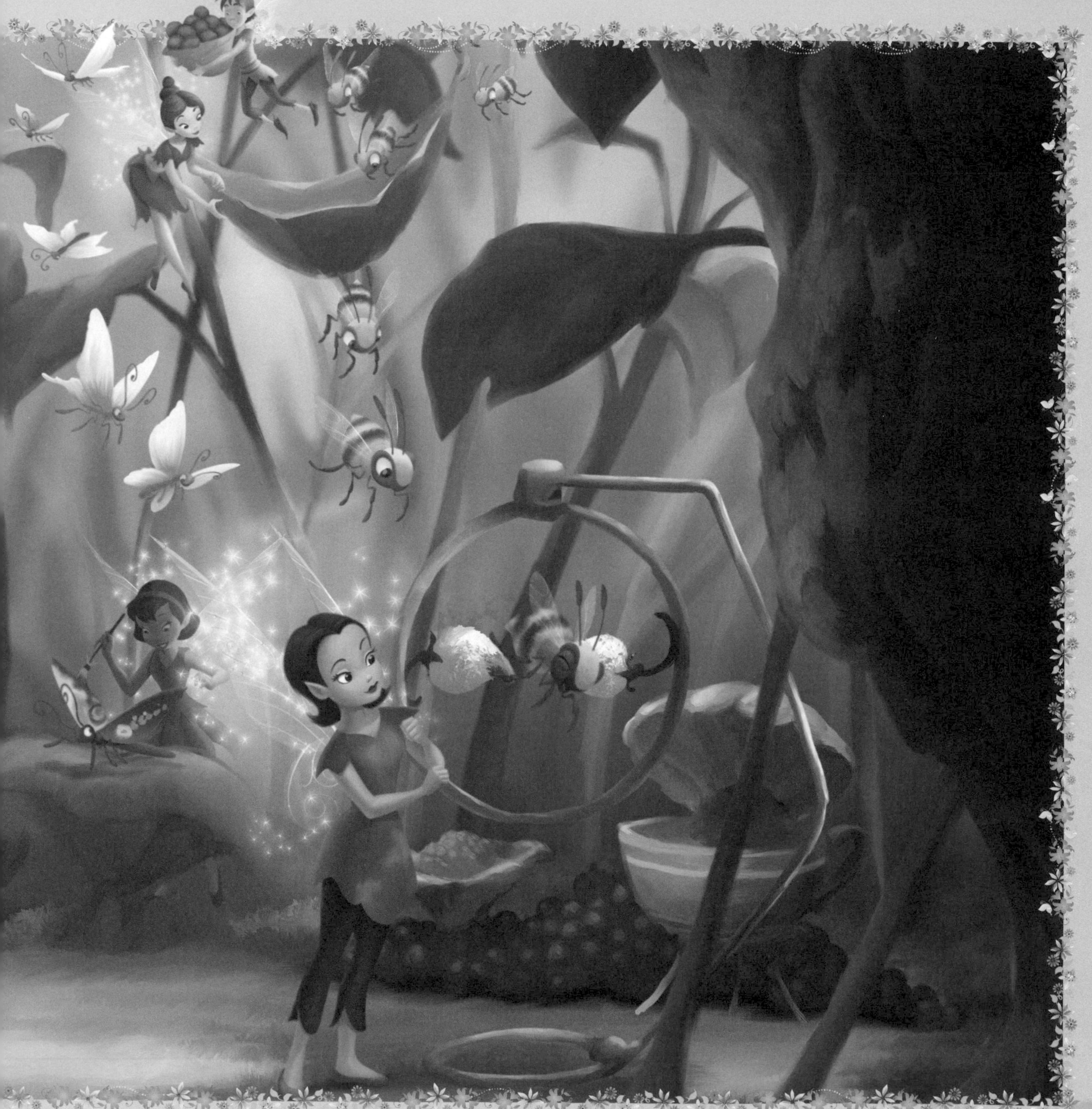

Memory game

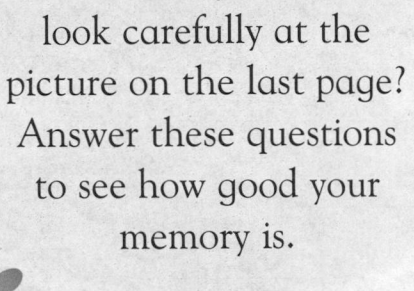

Did you look carefully at the picture on the last page? Answer these questions to see how good your memory is.

Don't look back at the picture until you've answered all the questions!

1. How many butterflies were fluttering in Fairy Camp?

....

2. What was one fairy transporting in a wheelbarrow?

....

3. Apart from Tink and Terence, how many other fairies did you count?

....

4. Were the ants blue in colour?

....

5. How many bees were buzzing in Fairy Camp?

....

6. What insect was being painted?

....

Answers on page 31

Shadows and light

Iridessa is bathing her flowers in beautiful sunshine.

Where there is light, a shadow is created too. Which shadow matches the picture of Iridessa?

A

B

C

D

E

F

Answers on page 31

21

Discovering humans

Tinker Bell is a very curious little fairy who loves to explore.

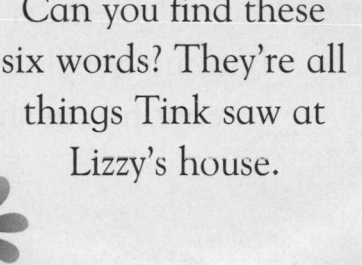

Can you find these six words? They're all things Tink saw at Lizzy's house.

LIZZY

CAR

DR GRIFFITHS

FAIRY HOUSE

BIRDCAGE

CAT

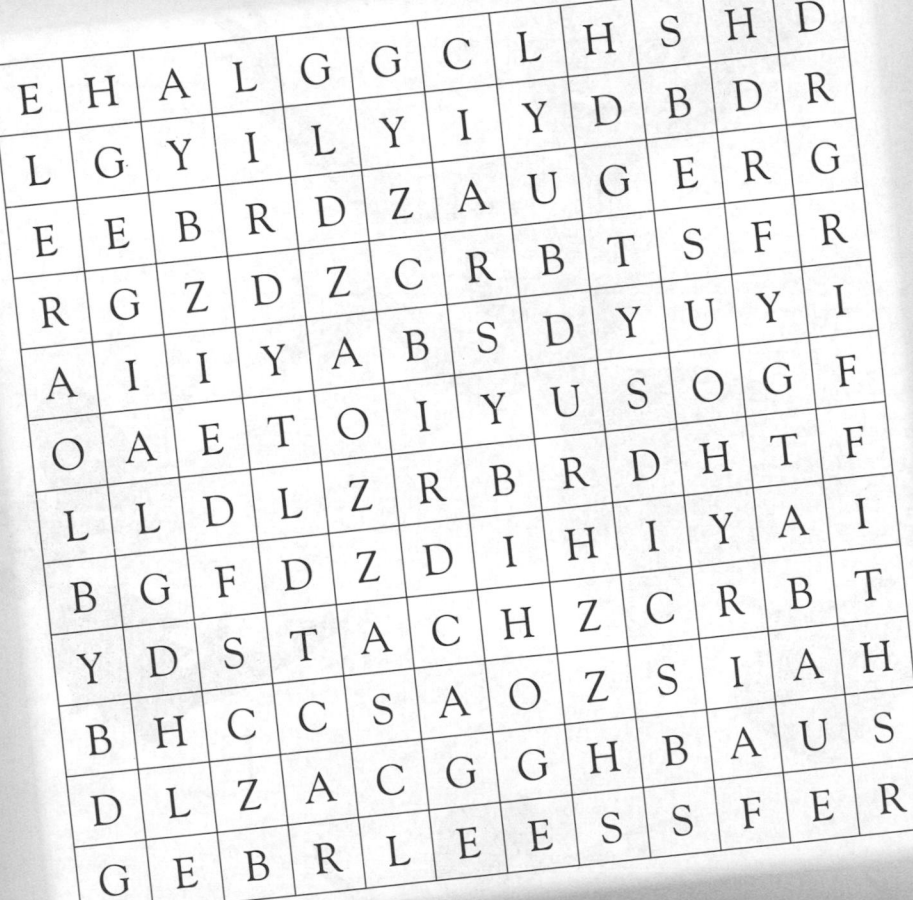

E	H	A	L	G	G	C	L	H	S	H	D
L	G	Y	I	L	Y	I	Y	D	B	D	R
E	E	B	R	D	Z	A	U	G	E	R	G
R	G	Z	D	Z	C	R	B	T	S	F	R
A	I	I	Y	A	B	S	D	Y	U	Y	I
O	A	E	T	O	I	Y	U	S	O	G	F
L	L	D	L	Z	R	B	R	D	H	T	F
B	G	F	D	Z	D	I	H	I	Y	A	I
Y	D	S	T	A	C	H	Z	C	R	B	T
B	H	C	C	S	A	O	Z	S	I	A	H
D	L	Z	A	C	G	G	H	B	A	U	S
G	E	B	R	L	E	E	S	S	F	E	R

22

Answers on page 31

This is Pixie Hollow

Tinker Bell teaches Lizzy, the little human girl, all about fairies.

Help Tink by colouring her picture of Pixie Hollow – the beautiful place where all the fairies live.

Story quiz

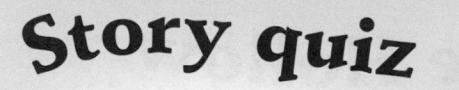

Have you flipped this book over and read the flitterific story yet?

If yes, see how much you can remember by completing this quiz. If not, come back later and see how many answers you can get right.

1. Which season are the fairies bringing to the mainland?

....

2. What is Vidia's fairy talent?

....

3. Which animal fairy gets a fright while she's painting a butterfly?

....

4. What is the name of the little girl that discovers Tinker Bell?

....

Answers on page 31

5. What do the other fairies build to help them travel in the rain?

....

6. What doesn't Dr Griffiths believe in?

....

7. What do the fairies use to make Lizzy fly?

....

8. What do the humans and fairies do together at the end of the story?

....

0-2

Your fairy knowledge is a little rusty, but don't worry! Read the story again and you'll soon be up to fast-flying speed on the fairies' greatest adventure.

3-5

You have a good knowledge of the fairy adventure. Read the story again and see if you can remember the ones you got wrong.

6-8

Lizzy would be proud! You are a fairy expert and you know this story very well!

Answers on page 31

Rosetta's flowers

Garden fairy Rosetta is colouring some beautiful flowers. How many flowers has she painted?

Answer

Answer on page 31

26

Beautiful colours

Rosetta is admiring her favourite flowers. The butterflies love them too.

Colour this picture.

Three in a row

Play this game with a friend!

Choose who will be Fawn and who will be Tinker Bell, then take turns to write F or T in the grid. The winner is the first player to fill three spaces in a row – horizontally, vertically or diagonally.

You can play three times on this page.

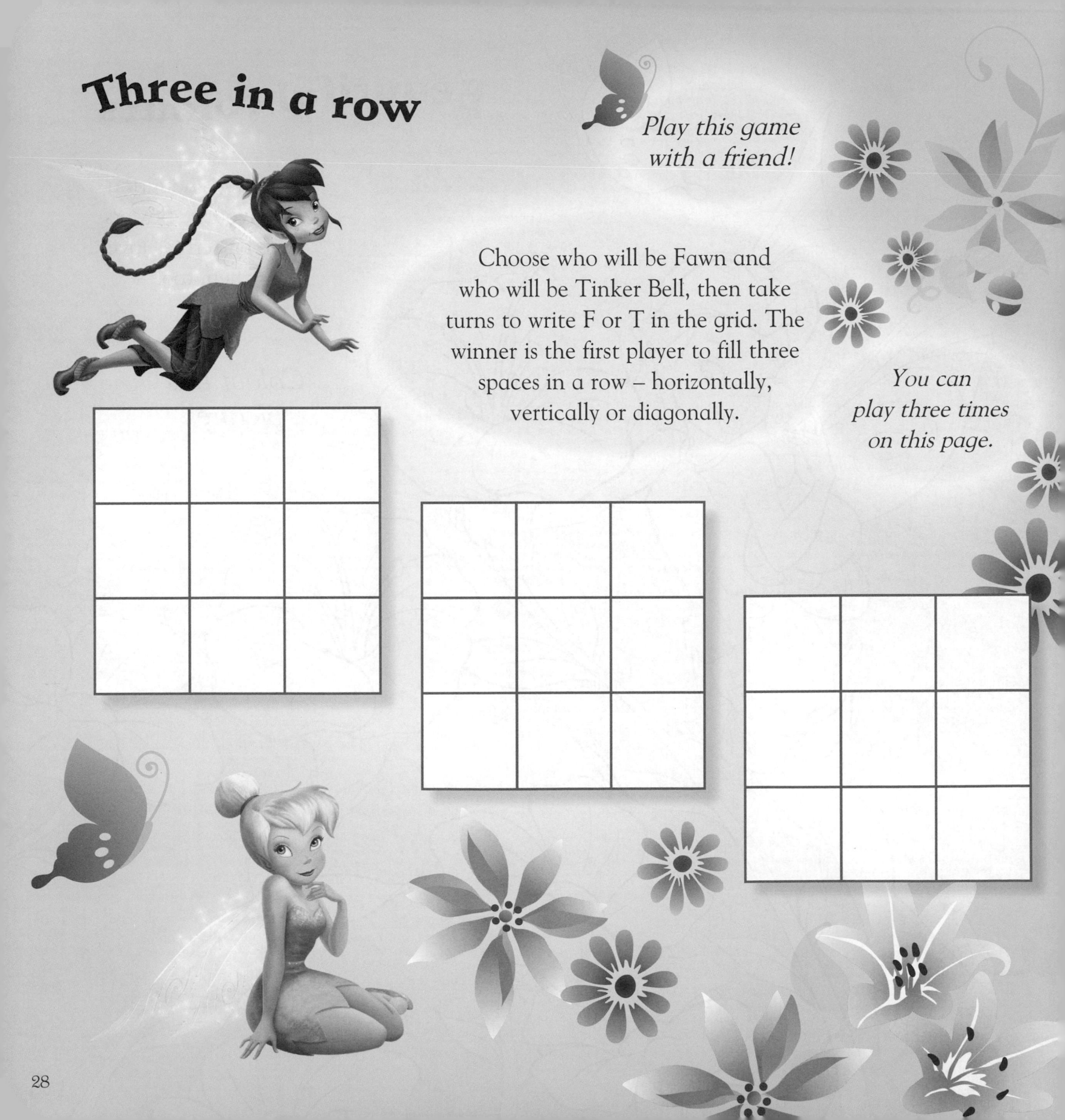

A fairy picnic

After all their adventures, Tink and Vidia have become good friends.

Colour this picture.

Which fairy are you?

1. **What's your favourite colour?**

   a. Yellow
   b. Orange
   c. Red
   d. Blue

2. **Which words best describe you?**

   a. Organized and smart
   b. Fun and a bit of a tomboy
   c. Sweet and a good listener
   d. Helpful and a little silly

3. **What kind of clothes do you like best?**

   a. Anything, as long as it sparkles!
   b. Anything comfortable
   c. Anything flowery
   d. Anything blue

4. **Which fun fairy thing would you most love to do?**

   a. Give fireflies their glow
   b. Talk to animals
   c. Help flowers to grow
   d. Train tadpoles to blow bubbles

5. **What would you choose as your fairy symbol?**

   a. A rainbow
   b. A mouse
   c. A flower
   d. A dewdrop

Mostly As

You're Iridessa!
As a light fairy you
would always know
how to look on the
bright side.

Mostly Bs

You're Fawn!
As an animal fairy
you would be able to
speak every animal
language.

Mostly Cs

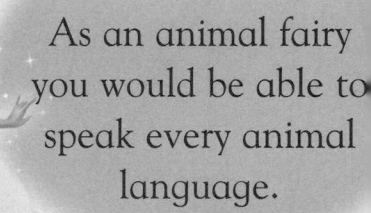

You're Rosetta!
As a garden fairy you
would make sure all
of the plants and trees
look beautiful.

Mostly Ds

You're Silvermist!
As a water fairy
you would love
hanging out by a
babbling brook.

Answers

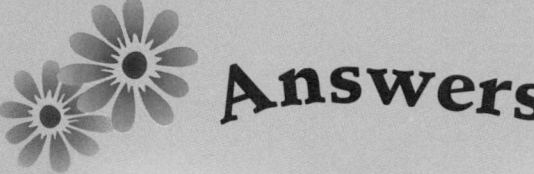

Page 4

Silvermist is a WATER fairy.

Iridessa is a LIGHT fairy.

Fawn is an ANIMAL fairy.

Rosetta is a GARDEN fairy.

Page 6

Page 8

4

Page 9

9 times

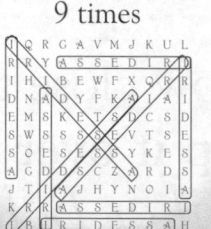

Page 11

Candle

Calendar

Cuckoo Clock

Cricket

Page 12

Page 17

C

Page 20

1. ten
2. bugs or insects
3. six
4. yes
5. six
6. butterfly

Page 21

D

Page 22

Pages 24-25

1. summer; 2. flying fast;
3. Fawn; 4. Lizzy; 5. a
boat; 6. fairies; 7. pixie
dust; 8. have a picnic

Page 26

There are
11 flowers

Now close the book,
flip it over and read
*Tinker Bell and the
Great Fairy Rescue* –
a **flitterific fairy story.**